THE
Archive Photographs
SERIES

HARROW

Harrow High Street, c.1867.

THE
Archive Photographs
SERIES

HARROW

Compiled by
Brian Girling

CHALFORD

First published 1996
Copyright © Brian Girling, 1996

The Chalford Publishing Company
St Mary's Mill, Chalford,
Stroud, Gloucestershire, GL6 8NX

ISBN 0 7524 0343 5

Typesetting and origination by
The Chalford Publishing Company
Printed in Great Britain by
Redwood Books, Trowbridge

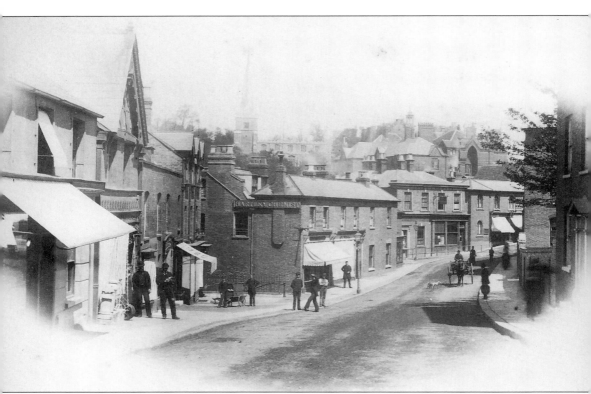

Harrow High Street, c.1895.

Contents

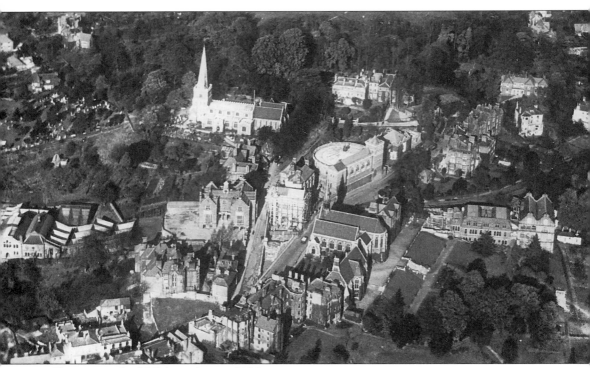

Harrow-on-the-Hill from the air, 1922.

Introduction

Say the word "Harrow" and the immediate thought is of one of the great public schools of England, but there is much more to Harrow than that. It is an ancient place with a documented history dating back to 767AD, and a 900-year-old church. It is also a populous London borough in the north-western sector of the city.

Harrow School was founded in 1572 when a charter was granted by Queen Elizabeth I to a wealthy country gentleman, John Lyon of Preston (to the east of Harrow) for the foundation of a free grammar school at Harrow-on-the-Hill. The school flourished through the centuries with new buildings being added around its historic heart, the partly seventeenth-century Old Schools. The Victorian age saw the erection of some of Harrow's finest buildings: the semi-circular Speech Room and the gothic style Vaughan Library and Chapel, designed by Gilbert Scott, while the present century's War Memorial building completed a stunning group of buildings. The school has produced seven British prime ministers including arguably its most famous old boy, Winston Churchill, together with a host of notable Englishmen including Lord Byron, Richard Brinsley Sheridan, Anthony Trollope, and Lord Shaftesbury.

Adjacent to the Old Schools is the ancient St Mary's church, whose tower and slender spire are seen from all over the borough rising above the thickly wooded slopes of Harrow Hill. The church was founded by Lanfranc, Archbishop of Canterbury, and consecrated in 1094 by Anselm, Lanfranc's successor. Some of the church's Norman stonework is still visible but the alterations of 900 years are evident. Gilbert Scott undertook a major restoration between 1846-49 and the present appearance of the church, with its impressive battlements and flint-faced walls, dates from that time. Byron's daughter, Allegra, is buried under the church porch as indicated by a commemorative tablet.

Harrow-on-the-Hill is a picturesque area of steeply graded streets filled with Victorian, Georgian, and houses. In spite of modern traffic, the atmosphere of yesteryear survives and the sense of other-worldliness is enhanced by the sight of the Harrow boys in their straw boaters and school masters in mortar boards and gowns. A 'mini green belt' of playing fields, open grassland and the school farm surround the Hill.

Harrow Hill was, for centuries, surrounded by miles of agricultural land but in 1837 the rural peace was disrupted by the wheezing and spluttering of the first steam railway in the district, together with a station at Wealdstone which served the Harrow area. At the northern foot of Harrow Hill the village of Greenhill was similarly disturbed in 1880 by the opening of an extension of the Metropolitan Railway, while at Roxeth (South Harrow) a new electric railway arrived in 1903. These railway links with London, some ten miles to the south east, set in motion the development of Harrow as a desirable suburb of the city. The increased accessibility of the Middlesex countryside soon ensured its popularity as a residential area, and the village of Greenhill become the shopping centre of the new Harrow, with shopping parades and cinemas to supply the entertainment of the electric age.

Following the First World War, London entered the period of greatest expansion in its history with immense housing estates spreading out from the city in all directions. To the north west some of the housing developments were promoted by the Metropolitan Railway who coined a new word, "Metroland", to symbolise a gracious life style with a house in the countryside and a fast train ride to work in the city. The new Metroland swallowed up old rural hamlets and villages like Kenton, Preston, Hooking Green, Rayners Lane and beyond as the seekers of the rural life style found the countryside evermore elusive among the housing schemes. Indeed, with their underground stations, red buses and cinemas, the new "Metrolanders" soon found themselves part of the city they thought they had left behind, albeit in much more attractive surroundings.

The inter-war years produced their own architectural style with gables, imitation half-timber and stained glass in the front door. "By-pass Tudor", some called it, but the shopping parades and cinemas were sometimes built in the ultra modern art deco style, especially at Rayners Lane where superb examples can still be seen.

By the 1980's Harrow town centre, the old Greenhill, was becoming rather run down and congested, but in 1987 the opening of the St Ann's indoor shopping mall brought a much-needed and most attractive amenity to the town, while the old St Ann's Road was pedestrianised and laid out with trees, flower beds and seating. At the time of writing a spectacular new shopping and leisure complex is being built which will considerably add to Harrow's standing as a shopping and commercial centre within Greater London.

Some of the changes of the past 130 years have been preserved in the photographs that comprise this book, and the author will always be pleased to hear from anyone who may have similar early photographs.

Brian Girling, 17 Devonshire Road, Harrow HA1 4LS

One
Harrow School

The Old Schools, Armstrong House and School Chapel, c.1890.

Old Schools and Church Hill, c.1920. As the name suggests this is the oldest part of Harrow School, dating in part from 1608. On the right is Armstrong House, almost hidden by its covering of ivy, and beyond can be seen the upper part of Church Hill House. Both were demolished and replaced by the War Memorial building, erected in memory of Old Harrovians who fell in the First World War.

Druries and Old Schools, c.1935. Demolition in 1929 of the old houses and shops adjoining the Old Schools revealed this fine view of the school steps, terraces and the boarding house, 'Druries', which dates from 1865.

Church Hill, 1904, with Old Schools and Armstrong House not yet hidden by creeper.

Thirty years later a comparison view shows the impressive War Memorial building with its steps and balustrades. This splendid addition to Harrow's fine array of buildings was designed by Sir Herbert Baker and the foundation stone was laid on 6 October 1921 by the Archbishop of Canterbury.

The school's roll call, or "Bill" as it is known, is taken in the school yard. A view from around 1908.

A busy scene on Church Hill, possibly at the beginning of term. The gates to the school yard are on the right and Headmaster's House in the High Street is in the distance.

The school's Officer Training Corps marching down Church Hill, c.1912. The house on the left was that of "Custos", the school's custodian. It was demolished in 1929.

The Fourth Form Room, c.1910. This is the school's oldest form room, dating from 1609. Notable are the oak panelled walls covered by the names and initials of old Harrovians carved into the woodwork. The earliest dates from 1660 and later ones include Byron, the poet; Anthony Trollope, the novelist; Sheridan, the dramatist; and Prime Ministers Palmerston, Peel and Spencer Perceval.

Harrow School chapel, c.1904. The beautiful flint and stone chapel was designed by Sir Gilbert Scott and consecrated on 1 November 1857. The newly built south door can be seen here.

Harrow School chapel, c.1880. This is the original west door of the chapel which opened right on to the noisy street causing disturbance during services. This was closed and new north and south doors built in 1903.

14

The Vaughan Library, 1906. Named after Rev Charles Vaughan, headmaster of Harrow 1845-1860, the Vaughan Library is another of Sir Gilbert Scotts' designs. The foundation stone was laid by Lord Palmerston on a very rainy 4 July 1861, which was Speech Day at the school. This photograph was also taken on Speech Day, with an orchestra playing on the green and Harrow boys resplendent in black top hats and tails.

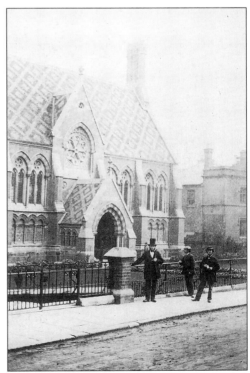

The brand new Vaughan Library - a photograph of the 1860s by the noted local photographer, Goshawk.

Speech Day, 1912. Continuing a tradition of Royal visits to Harrow School, King George V and Queen Mary came on 15 June 1912, driving to the school through a lavishly decorated High Street. Speech Room can be seen on the right, with Church Hill House beyond.

The steps and balustrades of the Memorial building provide an excellent viewpoint as the Duke and Duchess of York (later King George VI and Queen Elizabeth) visit Harrow School on 6 May 1929.

Headmaster's House from Church Hill, c.1912. Although this building is of 1840 vintage, there was a Headmaster's House here some two hundred years before that. Among numerous famous "old boys" of Headmaster's, including Sir Winston Churchill, was one of particular significance in a book such as this, Henry Fox Talbot, the inventor of the negative/positive photographic process that we use today. He was a boarder at Headmaster's in 1811 and was apparently already conducting malodorous chemical experiments while there.

Speech Room and the Art School, 15 June 1912. Speech Room dates from 1874 and the Art School, on the right, from 1896. The bunting is part of the decorations for the Royal visit.

The photographer provides temporary distraction from lessons as straw boatered Harrow boys emerge from their boarding house, Rendalls, c.1913. The house was built in 1853 at the top of Grove Hill.

The new Art School, Grove Hill, c.1913. A 5 mph speed limit sign warns of dangers ahead for the motorist on the steep winding Grove Hill, scene of Britain's first motoring fatality in 1899. A plaque nearby commemorates the incident, see page 49.

There is a fine tradition of cricket at Harrow, and the annual Eton-Harrow match is a considerable social function. Byron (the poet) was in the Harrow team in 1805. This Edwardian view taken from Lower Road shows a match in progress between Harrow School and Old Harrovians on the Sixth Form Ground, a setting almost unchanged in 90 years.

Harrow School football, c.1913. The football and rugby fields are in the eastern side of Harrow Hill.

Ducker, the school's bathing place, was in Sheepcote (later Watford) Road. The name is derived from "The Duck Puddle", a muddy swimming area created in 1809. It was improved to become the attractive place we see here, c.1912.

Ducker, c.1912. Note the delightful clock with its tiny roof and tower. Sadly, Ducker now lies derelict, bathing having been transferred to a new indoor swimming baths.

Two
St Mary's Church

HARROW CHURCH FROM MIDDLE ROAD.

St Mary's parish church sits atop the highest point of Harrow Hill as it has for the past 900 years. Much altered through the centuries, part of its Norman architecture can still be seen. Its tower and spire are a famous and prominent landmark, visible from all over the borough and from far beyond. This photograph was taken in 1908 from Middle Road and shows Church Fields and the Terrace, a famous viewpoint.

A rare early photograph of St Mary's church, c.1860, taken before the lychgate was built and the tower clock removed.

A snowy Edwardian scene with the lychgate in place. It was erected as a memorial to J.W. Cunningham, vicar of St Mary's from 1811-1861.

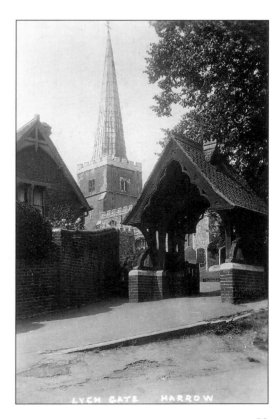

The tower and spire of St Mary's, c.1935, with the Victorian vicarage on the left.

Church Fields rise steeply towards St Mary's church, c.1925. Grazing sheep were once a familiar sight on this open grassland.

The church from the Fields, c.1930. Harrow was once noted for its towering elm trees, most of which succumbed to Dutch Elm Disease in the 1970's.

Church Fields, c.1907, with local children enjoying the tobogganing on the steep hillside.

UNUSUAL SPRING SCENE, HARROW, APRIL 24th 1908.

Church Fields, 24 April 1908. This icy Easter weekend produced conditions more appropriate to Christmas, but these children were happy enough with tobaggans and snowballs. Even so, Harrow escaped the worst of this freakish April weather - parts of Berkshire had a record 12 inches of lying snow.

The Church Terrace, c.1912. The Terrace is at the western end of the churchyard from where the ground falls away steeply to give a magnificent view over a vast stretch of Middlesex countryside. A direction pointer indicates distant landmarks like Windsor Castle and Winchester. Byron composed some of his earliest verse here while still at school.

Part of the view to the south west from St Mary's church, c.1907, showing Church Fields and cottage housing on the lower slopes of the hill. West Street is seen, centre of picture, with Victoria Terrace and Crown Street. Lower Road is at the top right. Modern housing has in recent years restricted some of the views in this part of Harrow Hill.

Three
Harrow-on-the-Hill

5. HIGH STREET, HARR

Harrow High Street is a delightfully old world thoroughfare that twists and climbs along the narrow ridge that dictates its course. The long vanished Crown & Anchor pub is seen to the left of this picture, c.1914, with Prentice & Chilmaid's drapery store, and A. Smith, the saddlers. Harrow School stores are here now. Beyond may be seen Headmaster's House, The Hill tearoom, and Harrow School bookshop.

Harrow High Street, c.1867. Many of the buildings shown on this historic photograph survive today including, on the left, the White Hart, which was an ale house until 1868 and is now a private house. The cottages in the centre of the picture had shop extensions built in their front gardens in the 1870s. The junction with West Street is seen with the town well. A drinking

fountain dated 1880 is there now. Visible in the distance are W. Smith's the corn chandlers, and Druries can be seen above the lower roof tops. St Mary's church, still with the tower clock, dominates the scene as it does today. School house, "Flambards" is on the right.

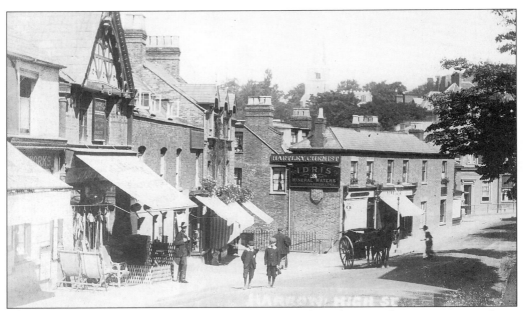

High Street, c.1904. The alterations of nearly 40 years from the preceding view are seen here, with the old White Hart building, by then a private house, and next door, Gage & Barker's hardware store.

High Street, October 1974. Moving on another 70 years, a further contrast is provided by this view taken when demolition revealed a half timbered wall, thought to be of sixteenth century origin. This ancient structure was later incorporated into the new buildings that arose here. They were similar in style to the demolished buildings, the street scene being well preserved. The noted tea rooms Ann's Pantry are seen here, occupying Gage & Barker's old shop.

High Street, c.1905. The shops in the centre of the picture, one of which contained the printing works of the local newspaper, The Harrow Gazette, have now been replaced by small office blocks. The saplings seen here have now grown to maturity.

High Street, c.1913, with school houses Bradbys on the left, and The Park on the right. The schoolmaster in mortar board and gown reads as he strolls in the middle of the road, a reminder of how peaceful the roads were in country towns like Harrow in the early part of the century.

The Kings Head Hotel, High Street, June 1905. The King was Henry VIII, in whose reign the hotel was founded, but this building is mostly of eighteenth and nineteenth century vintage following much rebuilding. The opulent decorations are in honour of a much later monarch, King Edward VII who, with Queen Alexandra, visited Harrow for Speech Day, 30 June 1905.

The Kings Head and The Green, c.1924. The Green has acquired some iron railings, but little else has changed from the earlier view. A 10 mph speed limit sign can be seen - the narrow High Street was hazardous for the motorist then as now.

32

The Royal Visit, 15 June 1912. Harrow was ablaze with colourful decorations once more as the town celebrated the arrival of King George V and Queen Mary for Speech Day. The banner referred to the previous royal visitors, King Edward VII, (see opposite page). This was the scene opposite the Kings Head.

The Royal Visit, 15 June 1912. A view from High Street towards London Road showing The Green. No doubt their Majesties were impressed by Harrow's decorative efforts.

Harrow Fire Station, c.1912. This fine Victorian building stands at the corner of Byron Hill Road opposite The Green, with the equally impressive bank built in 1889 to the left. The cottage, squeezed between them, disappeared when the Council Chamber was built in 1914 completing a splendid trio of buildings. The old Fire Station is now used as offices.

The New Motor Fire Engine, c.1910. Horse drawn appliances had previously been used, and the inadequacies of these were exposed in 1908 when there was a disastrous fire at Harrow School (see opposite page).

The Harrow Fire, 4 April 1908. Although the Fire Station was only a few yards away, the school house West Acre could not be saved as it erupted into a spectacular inferno that could be seen from all over the town. Poor water pressure on this hill-top location, leaky fire hoses, and antiquated fire appliances were all blamed for the completeness of the destruction, and matters were not helped by the strong wind of that night.

Only the shell of West Acre remained by the next morning, but remarkably the house was soon rebuilt, and still stands looking none the worse for its ordeal.

St Mary's church from Waldron Road, January 1963. This little by-way falls steeply from High Street to Crown Street, and before Victorian style houses were built here in the 1980's, this pleasant view could be seen. Waldron Road was named after a local builder.

Crown Street, 1963. An historic street, once called Hog Lane, that was, at the beginning of the century, full of shops and pubs serving the populous streets on the western side of Harrow Hill. When this picture was taken, the North Star pub on the corner of Waldron Road had already closed. It is now a private house, but it retains its tiled signs. The cottages on the right were originally shops but were rebuilt in 1988.

West Street, c.1912. Crampton's Tea Room and confectionery shop at 13 West Street occupied premises dating from 1557. There was a straw hat maker next door at number 15, and further up hill was Fletcher's cycle shop, where, in those early days of motoring, it was possible to buy petrol and oil for the car.

West Street, c.1960. Crampton's had become "The Teashop on the Hill", and the building had lost the imitation half timbering of the earlier view. More recent restoration has removed the rendering from the facade, and some of the original timber framing has been exposed.

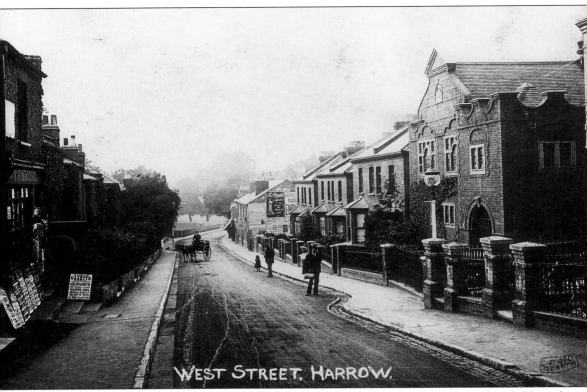

WEST STREET. HARROW.

West Street, c.1908. Looking down West Street's steep slope towards the cricket fields and Lower Road. On the left is Massey's, the newsagents and undertakers. Coffins were made in a building behind the shop. Behind the former Mission Hall, seen on the right, are the remains of one of Harrow's oldest structures, the fifteenth-century Pye Powder House. All these buildings still stand, and despite the modern traffic, the atmosphere of the country town that Harrow once was lingers here to this day.

Middle Road, c.1905. This was a typical mixture of cottages, pubs and shops on the lower slopes of Harrow Hill by Roxeth. On the right were Mr Bentley's Haircutting Rooms, and on the left by the wagon, the White Horse pub is seen. These old shops still stand but are now private dwellings.

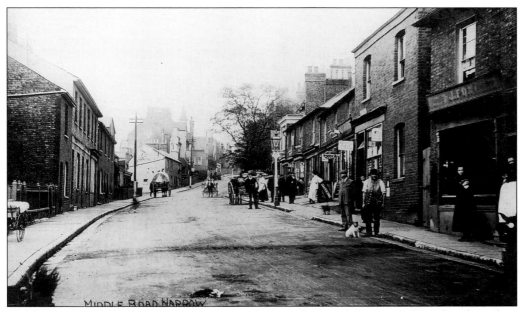

Middle Road, c.1908. Another busy scene in this populous road showing J. Fox's butchers shop on the right with Roxeth Post Office in the cottage beyond it. John Lyon School, built in 1876, can be seen in the distance. (A. & M. Back Collection).

Roxeth Hill, c.1910. Once called London Hill, this is now the busiest of the roads on the western side of Harrow Hill, but it was typically deserted in this Edwardian view taken from London Road.

Roxeth School, Roxeth Hill, 24 May 1912. A lively scene as the children of Roxeth School celebrate Empire Day. The school was built in 1851 in a rustic Gothic style.

Looking up Roxeth Hill, c.1913, with an impressive line up of local youth, no doubt having just been released from their labours at Roxeth School. To the left is Middle Road with the gabled Half Moon pub and the Salvation Army Hall beyond. See also page 97.

Harrow Cottage Hospital, c.1904. This attractive tile-hung house in Lower Road accommodated a nine-bed hospital, which opened in 1872. It was replaced in 1907 by a new hospital on Roxeth Hill.

Harrow Cottage Hospital on Roxeth Hill, photographed c.1908. Although Harrow now has a vast modern hospital at Northwick Park, this building is still in use.

The Cricket Fields, Bessborough Road, c.1912. A scene little changed in 80 years. The houses on the right are in Trafalgar Terrace and Nelson Road.

Bessborough Road in 1912 was a narrow winding road, much as it is today. With cricket fields on both sides, it retains its attractiveness. Through the trees, the weatherboarded Roxeth Farm, one of Harrow's finest examples of domestic architecture, is just visible. The horse trough now resides on the opposite pavement, and the seat was used to watch the cricket. Note the very informative lamp, illuminating signs for three roads and two railway stations.

Sudbury Hill, c.1912. This is a continuation of London Road and descends the southern side of Harrow Hill to Sudbury.

Sudbury Hill by South Hill Avenue, c.1912. This useful resting place was provided half way up the steep southern slope of Harrow Hill, with seats and a fine view of Horsenden Hill and beyond to the distant North Downs of Surrey. The roof of the former Harrow School Sanatorium can be seen.

South Hill Avenue, Mount Park Estate, c.1908. This is an attractive residential area on the southern side of Harrow Hill, with many large Victorian and Edwardian properties.

The Toll-gate, South Hill Avenue, c.1912. The approach to the Mount Park Estate is guarded to this day by one of London's few surviving toll gates.

Roxborough Path from St Mary's churchyard, c.1875. Through the kissing gate, the dusty pathway was soon to develop into Roxborough Park with its large houses and leafy gardens. The Church of Our Lady & St Thomas was built at the bottom of the hill in 1894 and all the distant

countryside we see here was eventfully covered in housing as Harrow transformed itself into a suburb of London.

Roxborough Park, c.1912. The changes of 40 years are seen from a similar viewpoint to that of the preceding photograph. Still visible are the kissing gate and the large Victorian house at the corner of Roxborough Park and Roxborough Avenue. The old pathway through open pasture has become a proper road, and the scene has the well-wooded aspect we know today. The old kissing gate has since been replaced by more mundane bollards.

Edwardian fashions on view in Peterborough Road, c.1910. This road was created in 1879 to allow a gentler descent of Harrow Hill than its neighbour, the steep and dangerous Grove Hill.

The Grove Hill Motor Accident. Mr E.R. Sewell, a representative of the Daimler Motor Company made history on 25 February 1899 when he became the first motorist to be killed in a motor accident in this country. Driving a Daimler Wagonette with five passengers on a demonstration run from Westminster, Mr Sewell and his party enjoyed lunch at the Kings Head before setting off on the return run to London. Whether the lunch was good enough to inspire recklessness, we will never know, but in any event, Mr Sewell decided to put the wagonette through its paces with a turn of speed on the steep gradients and sharp bends of Grove Hill, much to the alarm of his passengers. The descent was accomplished, but still travelling at speed, the vehicle took the right turn into Lowlands Road and disaster struck as one of the back wheels shed its solid rubber tyre. The combined weight of six people and a heavy machine proved too much for the somewhat flimsy wooden wheel, which collapsed throwing everyone out onto the road. Mr Sewell died within minutes, and one of the passengers some days later. The photograph shows the wagonette facing back up Grove Hill.

Grove Fields, c.1912. The green northern slopes of Harrow Hill still has this fine viewpoint over the modern town. The Edwardian developments of Whitehall, Lansdowne, and Lowlands Roads are seen here, with Harrow-on-the-Hill station behind the trees to the right. This remains a very pleasant part of Harrow, although newer high rise buildings in the town centre restrict some of the views. The hills on the horizon are at Pinner and Northwood to the left, and Harrow Weald to the right.

Whitehall Road and Lansdowne Road, c.1912. These two roads, attractively located beside Grove Fields, remain little changed in appearance today.

Lowlands Road, c.1912. To the left are Grove Fields and to the right, part of the former Lowlands estate that became Lowlands Recreation Ground in the 1920's. Also seen are J. T. Garrett's, the gardeners shop by the approach to Harrow-on-the-Hill station. Timber yards and DIY premises flourished here in later years before giving way to some of Harrow's more agreeable modern office blocks.

Recreation Ground, Harrow   103655

When Lowlands, a large private estate in Lowlands Road was sold early in the century, part of its well-wooded grounds were used as a recreation ground. A feature was the small pond we see here, c.1922, highly popular with the young and their model ships. The pond was subsequently filled-in, but the greenery remains a local attraction. The original Lowlands House still stands, and forms part of Greenhill College.

Lowlands Road from Grove Hill, c.1910, showing the entrance to Lowlands House.

Four

The Town Centre

The arrival in 1880 of the Metropolitan Railway at the pretty village of Greenhill began a process that was eventually to transform it into the modern town centre of Harrow. Its principal street, Greenhill Lane soon became lined with new shops, and it acquired a new name to reflect its increasingly urban status, Station Road. This view, c.1912 shows the beginning of Station Road by the Metropolitan Railway bridge. The sign pointed to what was then the main station entrance off Lowlands Road. As the town centre developed, the emphasis moved away to the station's opposite side in College Road. Shops were soon erected over the bridge itself.

THE COLISEUM

PHONE: HARROW 0266

General Manager : H. Lennox.　　　　*Resident Manager* : W. H. Bird.

Continuous

Performance

from 2 p.m.

except

where

specially

mentioned

Prices
from
Monday to
Friday
9d., 1/3
1/6, 1/10
2/4 and
3/6
including tax

Saturdays
and
Bank
Holidays
9d., 1/3
1/10, 2/4
and 3/6
including tax

Organist - - - EDWARD FARLEY

REVIEW OF ATTRACTIONS
FEBRUARY 1935

Western Electric
SOUND SYSTEM

Although there were already several cinemas in Harrow, new standards of luxurious entertainment were set following the opening of the 2000 seat Coliseum on 11 October 1920 by Harrow's MP, Oswald Mosely. These familiar twin domes were to dominate Station Road for the next 38 years, until closure in 1958. The Coliseum was converted into a theatre in 1939. The Iceland supermarket occupies the site now. This is a programme from February 1935 with such delights as "The Last Gentleman" with Robert Arliss, and "Bulldog Drummond Strikes Back" starring Ronald Colman.

When first built, the Coliseum was an imposing sight standing in isolation among the private houses and gardens that still occupied the east side of Station Road. The road was still narrow, but the Coliseum set the new building line adopted by later shopping developments. This postcard, sent in 1922, has the message "This is our cinema ... the best of the town". The trees are in the garden of "Dunwich", see below.

"Dunwich", the private house occupied by Dr W.S. Darby stood adjacent to the Coliseum and was photographed c.1920 from its garden which extended back to Lyon Road. Station Road is seen beyond the trees with Sainsbury's shop and Barclays Bank at the corner of College Road. (A. & M. Back Collection)

Station Road, c.1906. The road was rapidly taking shape as Harrow's shopping centre, but to the right large private houses still stood. A view taken before the Coliseum was built.

Station Road c.1928, as seen from Gayton Road with the Coliseum and shopping parades on both side of the road. Home-made cakes were an attraction at the Blue Bird Tearoom on the left.

HARROW. STATION RD. SHEWING OBSERVER OFFICE.

Station Road looking north from College Road, c.1920. The distinctive gabled shopping parade on the left, once called The Market, dates from the beginning of the century. Many Harrovians will remember Somerton's ladies fashion shop on the corner of College Road, which survived until the 1970s. The cottages in the centre of this view were surviving remnants of the old Greenhill village; two of them are still with us today. The shops on the right were once known as The Broadway, and the glazed roof covered a walkway leading to the Harrow (later Broadway) Cinema which stood behind the shops. Note the rather unusual vertical sunblinds.

The Havelock Arms, Station Road, June 1911. This was one of the old pubs of Greenhill village that survived to quench the thirsts of Harrow's latterday shoppers. To the left can be seen the offices of the well-known local newspaper, The Harrow Observer, and in their window can be seen pictures of King George V and Queen Mary. It is in their honour that the patriotic display of flags and decorations has been set up, for it was Coronation time. Their Majesties were crowned in Westminster Abbey on 22 June 1911.

Opposite: Station Road and Greenhill Parade, c.1924. The Westminster Bank building with its distinctive brickwork dates from 1915. The shops of Greenhill Parade are on the right. Copious droppings in the road would indicate that the motor had not entirely superseded the horse by the mid-twenties!

Station Road looking south by College Road, c.1924. Barclays Bank is still on the corner of College Road, but in premises rebuilt in the 1970s. The neighbouring Sainsbury's shop has long gone. On the right were the shops of John Hall, the drapers, and Somertons, their window displays protected by sunblinds. Recent years have seen an improvement in the environment here with tree planting, and decorative brick paving, together with partial pedestrianisation.

Harrow Technical & Art School, Station Road, was built in 1902, and is pictured here c.1918. Classes taken here included Art and Technical Drawing, Plumbing and Carpentry, also Domestic Science and Languages. The school flourished through the decades, but the building was demolished in 1970 following the school's removal to a new campus at Northwick Park.

The Technical School, c.1905, a view taken before a new wing was added in 1907. Three of the four houses we see here still survive, and can be seen behind the shops that were built in their front gardens.

Greenhill Parade; Station Road and St Ann's Road, c.1911. Here was one of the dairy shops of One Hundred Elms Farm, "Special Cows Kept for the Nursery and Invalids". This was a well-known local firm with branches at West Street, Headstone Road and Pinner High Street. On the top floor were Charles Praeger's Dental Chambers, where, in those pre-National Health Service days, a troublesome molar could be extracted by a "Painless American Process" for 2s. (10p).

One Hundred Elms Farm, Sudbury, c.1911. The Harrow shops were supplied from this establishment, one of numerous dairy farms in the countryside between Harrow and London earlier this century.

Another of the highly popular shops in the newly built Greenhill Parade was that of R. & J. Elias who occupied numbers 2 and 3 in St Ann's Road. This picture was taken around 1905 when the windows were crammed with merchandise of all kinds, including "Old Invalid Port at 2s. 6d. (12p) per bottle, and a 40 piece "Elegant Tea Service" for 7s. 11d. Also on offer were "Ostend Rabbits". R. & J. Elias operated a home delivery service using a very odd looking three-wheeled motor.

Opposite: Sopers store was founded in 1914 and is seen here from St John's Road in 1963. The new extension on the site of the Marquis of Granby is seen on the right, and eventually the whole frontage was rebuilt in a similar style. The shop is now a branch of Debenhams.

Station Road from St John's Road, c.1908. On the left is the eighteenth-century Marquis of Granby pub, with H. Botten & Sons, the blacksmiths beyond. The pub was rebuilt in 1925 and finally closed in 1960 when the site was used for an extension to Harrow's popular department store, Sopers. This is all now part of the teeming heart of modern Harrow's shopping centre. (A. & M. Back Collection)

Station Road, 1918. This formidable looking beast was "Bobby", a Tank Bank that visited Harrow towards the end of the First World War as part of a nationwide fundraising drive for the war effort, by selling War Saving Certificates. On the wall of the old smithy in the background are film posters for the long vanished Harrow Cinema, which stood behind Station Road near the Technical School. On 30 April 1912, the Harrow Cinema gave two special charity performances in aid of "Sufferers of the Titanic Disaster".

The Tank Bank progresses through Station Road past the Marquis of Granby. Also seen is a builder's board proclaiming the development of "The Promenade", a terrace of shops that was to extend the existing Greenhill Parade northwards. All the background shown would, in time, be occupied by Sopers huge department store, and then by Debenhams. (See preceding page)

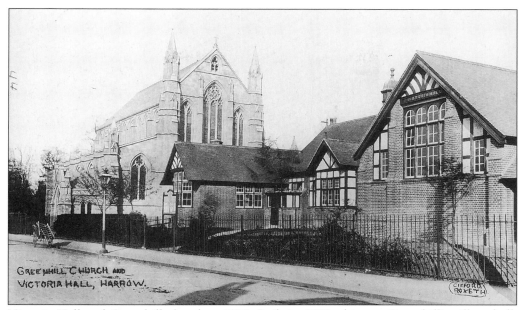

Victoria Hall and Greenhill church, c.1906. Built in 1888, this was Greenhill's village hall, occupying a site at the corner of St John's Road and Station Road, opposite the Marquis of Granby. A new Victoria Hall was built in Sheepcote Road during the 1960s, together with new shops on the old hall site, all but obscuring this view of Greenhill church.

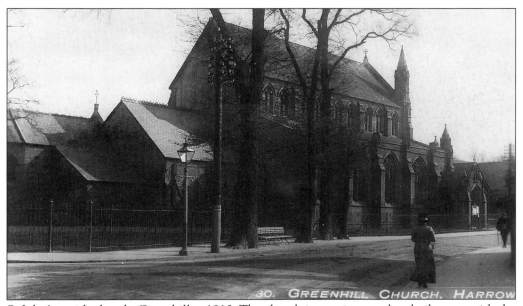

St John's parish church, Greenhill, c.1910. The church is seen in a partly rebuilt state, with the small scale Victorian part in a dilapidated state to the left, and the newer Gothic style part to the right. The rebuilding was completed in the early 1920s, and consecration occurred in 1925.

Station Road, 4 August 1906. There was excitement aplenty in Greenhill as a water main fractured spectacularly at the junction of Station Road and Sheepcote Road. Despite this watery onslaught, the trees to the right, in front of Greenhill's Manor House, were to survive for another 30 years until the Granada cinema and Manor Parade shops were built.

Sheepcote Road from Station Road, c.1904. By comparison with the previous picture, a tranquil scene outside Greenhill's seventeenth-century Manor House, which was reached through the white gate. All was swept away for the building of the Granada cinema and adjoining shops in 1937. Part of the original St John's church is on the right.

Sheepcote Road looking towards Station Road, c.1907. This road was already fully developed with spacious houses, but still had a peaceful look when compared with this view today with its relentless through traffic. Almost all these houses have gradually disappeared, and there are large blocks of flats on the right.

Early in the century there were numerous private schools accommodated in Harrow's larger houses. This was St Margaret's, an exclusive girls school which occupied The Crofts and its extensive grounds in Station Road, opposite Fairholme Road. This was the tennis lawn, c.1906, showing a donkey drawn mower, no doubt a favourite with the young ladies.

The Gymnasium at St Margaret's School, c.1906. A lengthy shopping parade was built here after the school vacated The Crofts in 1936.

The Metropolitan and Great Central Railway station, Harrow-on-the-Hill, c.1910. The station opened on 2 August 1880 with two platforms, and was remodelled in 1908 to provide two more. A complete rebuilding in 1938-39 provided a new ticket hall above the tracks, and the six platforms that exist today.

The modest architecture of the original Harrow-on-the-Hill station, c.1912. This was the main entrance off Lowlands Road. In the distance can be seen the shops of T.D. & A.R. Peacey, the estate agents, and Brentnall & Cleland, the coal merchants. There is a car park there now, and there are steep stairs up to the station entrance.

The Roxborough Hotel, College Road, c.1911. The Victorian Roxborough Hotel was a prominent feature at the western entrance to Harrow town centre, until its recent replacement by the massive Aspect Gate office block. The adjoining shops were the first to be built in College Road, but most are now offices.

A residential College Road from Roxborough Bridge, c.1908, showing undeveloped land all the way to Harrow-on-the-Hill station. There was a path from College Road to the station. (A. & M. Back Collection)

College Road by Clarendon Road, c.1910. These Victorian houses survived until the 1980s when the site was used for the vast Queens House office blocks. A new road, an extension of Kymberley Road, now emerges into College Road, centre of picture, and beyond, a dismal row of office blocks extend as far as Headstone Road.

College Road, 1965. To the left were the single-storey shops that fronted Harrow-on-the-Hill station. These were swept away in the 1970s to make way for Harrow Bus Station and an office block of brutal hideousness which formed the new station entrance. On the right can be seen the last of College Road's schools, Heathfield. There is a Marks & Spencers there now, part of the new St Ann's Centre.

College Road, 1974, showing Webb's Garden Centre and the shops that were soon to be developed as Harrow Bus Station. The house on the far right on the Clarendon Road corner can be seen on the early photograph on page 71.

College Road from Station Road, c.1957. The Green Line "T" type coach was on the long withdrawn route 703 to Wrotham, Kent. Somerton's is seen on their corner to the right, and although College Road was illuminated by fluorescent lamps on ugly concrete columns, the traffic island still had an old gas lamp.

College Road looking towards Station Road, c.1952. Every building shown here has gone including Harrow Baptist church; the old Post Office, and the small shops to the left where St Ann's Shopping Centre now is.

College Road from a similar viewpoint, c.1970, showing the new Post Office on the right. This opened in January 1962. Vanished landmarks on the left include Grange Furniture store; Abbey National Building Society; and the bay windowed Heathfield School. Their sites were all used for the St Ann's Centre, opened on 18 November 1987 by the Princess of Wales.

Clarendon Road, 1974. These were originally three pairs of semi-detached houses that were later fitted with shop fronts as Harrow's shopping facilities expanded. For many years this was a delightful street of small specialist shops until demolition in the mid seventies and replacement with the faceless slab block that is Queens House.

The Royal Oak from Clarendon Road, 1974. Buses no longer pass this old pub as it is now in Harrow's attractive St Ann's pedestrian precinct. The Adams furniture shop on the left once housed what was in 1912, Harrow's largest cinema, the Harrow Empire & Picturedrome. The new St George's Centre is currently being built on the Adams site, and this will include a new multi-screen cinema complex, marking a return of the cinema to this location after an absence of some 70 years.

St Ann's Road, c.1909. The splendid St Ann's Shopping Centre was opened in 1987 on the site of these Victorian houses and shops. To the left was the Greenhill Laundry, and to the right can be seen the newly built premises that were to become the Harrow Empire & Picturedrome, and later, Adams furniture store.

This was St Ann's Road, c.1955, as most Harrovians will remember it, crammed with small shops and houses. The whole street has been completely rebuilt with new shops, trees, seats and flower beds. Pedestrianisation has also added to this most agreeable shopping environment.

St Ann's Road near Greenhill Road (now Havelock Place), c.1912. These were some of the original small shops of St Ann's Road including the long established F.C. Guppy, the jeweller, and Hooper's Domestic Fancy Stores. "Veritas Mantles" in W. Cole's shop on the right remind us of the gas lighting of the period.

St Ann's Road from Station Road, c.1960. A typically congested road as it was before pedestrianisation. On the right was the former Greenhill Parade with Wyman's the newsagents at No. 4. See page 61 for another picture of this shop, taken when it was One Hundred Elms Dairy. Greenhill School was to the left behind the trees. The charming statue "Katie" now occupies a position in the foreground of this view.

Springfield Road, c.1907. This was another of the town centre roads of small shops and houses that has undergone drastic alteration as Harrow rebuilds its town centre. All the shops on the right together with those on the left up to the detached house were swept away with the construction of a new town centre relief road, Greenhill Way. The detached house was on the corner of Amersham Road, and although this house (now a shop) still stands by the busy new road, Amersham Road disappeared from the map completely. The distant houses and shops still survive in what is left of Springfield Road. The new road replaced St Ann's Road as an east-west traffic route. (A. & M. Back Collection)

Kymberley Road from Clarendon Road, c.1907. These pleasant tile-hung houses gave their sites for another part of the Queens House offices and the new link road to College Road. The more distant houses were replaced by a multi-storey car park.

An "RT" type bus in Kymberley Road by Springfield Road passes soon to be demolished property including the well-remembered Kay's secondhand shops. After demolition, there was an open-air car park here as planners agonised over what become known as "The Island Site". Now, the spectacular St George's Shopping and Leisure Complex is in course of erection.

St Kilda's Road, c.1905. These terraces survive in what is now a pleasantly tree-lined street, but the distant view of Harrow Hill has been obscured by the bulk of the new St George's Centre. Amersham Road is seen in the distance.

Byron Road, c.1907. The creation of Greenhill Way swept away the four house terrace on the right, including George Gooderson's lavishly windowed builders shop.

Headstone Road looking north, c.1908. There is little to suggest in this tranquil scene that by the mid-nineties it would become one of the busiest traffic junctions in the town, with the elevated roundabouts of Roxborough Bridge reached from ramps to the left, and Greenhill Way off to the right. Kymberley Road is on the right and the houses on the left were replaced with Bradstowe House, the DSS offices.

The Olympic Games came briefly to Harrow on 24 July 1908 when the Marathon, run from Windsor to the new White City Stadium, passed through the town. Here we see C. Hefferson, a South African runner, crossing Roxborough Bridge. He finished in second place.

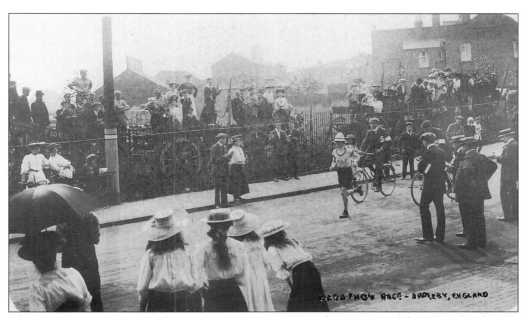

The Marathon, Pinner Road, 24 July 1908. Harrovians cheer on Appleby of England as he approached Roxborough Bridge. Behind the railings, one of Brentnall & Clelands coal wagons gave a grandstand viewpoint for spectators.

Bromley's Stores, c.1907. This is one of a little group of shops that stood in Bessborough Road by Roxborough Bridge until swept away by road widening in the 1980s. This postcard was sent by the shopkeeper in 1907, and in the message he refers to holiday plans in Brighton. "Harrow is such a very quiet place we feel we would like to see a little life".

Harrow Cycle Carnival, Easter 1908. Revellers gather for a photograph in Harrow Recreation Ground, Pinner Road having completed a "Grand Fancy Costume Cycle Procession" through the streets of Harrow. This was a very successful event in spite of frequent snow and hail showers. The old wooden cricket pavilion was recently burnt down, but soon rebuilt in 1994.

More fancy costumes at the carnival. Prizes were awarded for the best costumes, the winner being a Mr Ritches who won a clock. The building on the right was an indoor rifle range.

Empire Day 1908.

Patriotic fervour as the youth of Harrow celebrates Empire Day, 24 May 1908, with this parade in Pinner Road on the way to a ceremony by the flag in Harrow Recreation Ground. These houses are now occupied by Harrow Hotel, and the elevated Roxborough Bridge roundabouts are to the right. This old postcard was written to a lady in Cheshire by someone called Tom who invites her to find me on the other side".

Five

The Growing Suburb

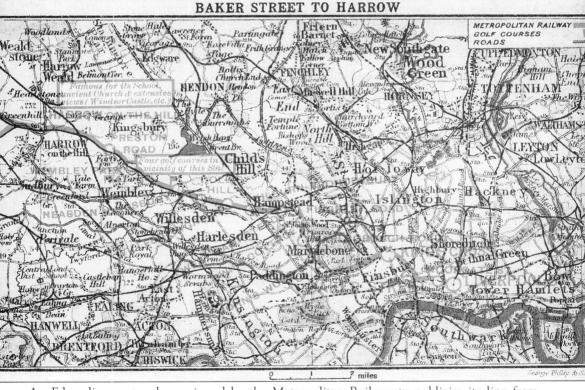

An Edwardian postcard map issued by the Metropolitan Railway to publicise its line from Harrow to Baker Street and the City of London. These were the early days of the Metroland dream of a house in the countryside and a fast electric train to work in the City. Until then, Harrow was expanding slowly as did countless other country towns, but after the First World War, the vast new housing estates of the new Metroland began to cover much of agricultural Middlesex in a frenzy of development that welded it forever to the capital city.

Sussex Road, c.1907. The Edwardian years saw a gradual expansion of the town, and to the west of the old Greenhill area, the Belmont Park Estate began to be laid out along Pinner Road. One of the builders of the estate, C. & F. Westcott, issued this postcard to advertise its new houses in Sussex Road. Note the unmade state of the road and pavement. This area is popularly referred to as "The County Roads", for the obvious reason that all the roads are names after English Counties.

Correspondence

ATTRACTIVE WELL-BUILT VILLAS
SITUATED IN
SUSSEX RD. (*bottom of Devonshire Rd.*)
Pinner Rd., HARROW-ON-THE-HILL.

Ten Minutes from Metropolitan and Great Central Station, from which station through trains are run to the City (30 min.) and the West-End (21 min.) every Ten Minutes.

Accommodation consists of attractive six-foot Entrance Hall, Two Reception Rooms about 12ft. 6in. by 11ft. 6in., Two Bedrooms of similar size and One Smaller Bedroom 7ft. by 9ft., Good Bathroom with Bath and Lavatory Basin and Hot Linen Cupboard. Combined specially-planned Kitchen and Scullery, fitted with every convenience. Tiled Forecourt and Verandah at back. Good Gardens front and back.

Price, Freehold, £380 ; Leasehold, £265.

Lease 99 years, Ground Rent £5 5s. per annum, or £25 deposit, balance as rent about £28 per annum including ground rent. Total cost of house would be £34 per annum or 13s. per week, including monthly instalments, ground rent and rates. The houses can be seen at any time, but a postcard making an appointment would much oblige.

Messrs. C. & F. WESTCOTT, Builders,
"Shanklin," Devonshire Road, or 2, Dorset Road,
Devonshire Road, Pinner Road, Harrow.

The reverse of the postcard shown above, with house prices that seem unbelievable today. The proximity to the station was always a good selling point.

Oxford Parade, Pinner Road, c.1912. New shops for the Belmont Park Estate, including a branch of the W.H. Cullen, Allen's Shoe Shop, Burwood Dairy, and F.W. Olney, the fruiterers who had several branches in Harrow. The trees were all that remained of the hedgerows that formerly bordered the fields along Pinner Road. Oxford Road is on the left.

DAVIS'S MODEL BAKERY 136. PINNER RD, HARROW.
Have you tried our - Bread and Cakes, if not, why not.

J. Davis's Model Bakery, Oxford Parade, Pinner Road, c.1910.

The temporary corrugated iron church of St George, Headstone, was built in 1907 to serve the new western suburbs of Harrow. Pinner View is in the foreground, with Hide Road to the left and Longley Road in the distance.

St George's, Headstone, c.1912. The foundation stone of the new permanent church was laid by, Adeline, Duchess of Bedford on 22 October 1910, and consecration took place on 7 October 1911. The architect was J.S. Alder, and original plans included a tower, which was unfortunately never built.

A rare Edwardian view of a somewhat dilapidated Honeybun Farmhouse, which stood in Bessborough Road opposite Roxborough Avenue. One of Harrow's first council housing estates was laid out on the former farmlands in the early twenties.

115242. Lascelles Avenue, Harrow.

The Honeybun Estate, c.1923. This is Lascelles Avenue, the central road through the estate with its smart new houses. It is now a main road, but its grassy verges and plentiful tress give it a very pleasant aspect.

As Harrow grew in the inter-war years, the expansion of London itself was even more rapid. The scale of the massive housing estates between London and Harrow is illustrated by this view of Preston and Kenton to the east of Harrow, c.1922. The Metropolitan railway line to Baker Street, and the Great Central Line to Marylebone are in the foreground.

These new houses in Metroland cost £700 freehold in the 1920s. This was New College Estate, built on the fields of New College Farm between Wealdstone and Belmont.

North Harrow is entirely a creation of the twentieth century, following the opening of the Metropolitan Railway station on 22 Mary 1915. This previously rural area had been known as Hooking Green. A view of the new shopping centre of Station Road and Pinner Road, c.1929, shows popular chain stores like Stowell's, Express Dairies and United Dairies already in evidence, with new shops as yet unoccupied in the distance. On the right, the now vanished landmark of the Embassy cinema was a popular amenity until its replacement by a Safeway supermarket in 1963. A leafy cul-de-sac close by preserves the old name of Hooking Green.

Broadway Parade, Station Road, North Harrow, c.1929. North Harrow station with its wooden street level ticket office is seen in the distance by the large tree. A new station entrance and another row of shops were built in 1930.

Station Road from Imperial Drive, North Harrow, c.1929. The shops now on the south side of the station had yet to be built. The wooden huts were sales offices for Cutler's, one of the more prolific local house builders.

Headstone Lane, North Harrow, c.1906. Now a busy main road, Headstone Lane was a peaceful rural by-way before the arrival of the housing estates of North Harrow.

Additional bus services were needed to connect the new housing estates with shopping centres and railway stations, and this London General Omnibus Company "S" type working route 353 duly obliged. The route ran from Pinner to North Harrow station, via Headstone Lane and Hatch End. A view at the Red Lion, Pinner in the late 1920s.

Rayners Lane in the early 1930s still had a muddy rural look about it, but there were builder's boards on all sides, and the first shops had appeared by Village Way; another new suburb was being born. The slope up to the old wooden Rayners Lane station can be seen in the distance.

Waverley Road, Rayners Lane, c.1938. Typical Metroland houses of the 1930s.

The Metropolitan and Piccadilly Underground station, Rayners Lane, c.1939. This fine building, designed by R.H. Uren, opened on 8 August 1938, replacing a primitive wooden structure of 1906 vintage, once known as Rayners Lane Halt. The old gas lamp contrasts with the modernity of the electric age.

The main road through the vast new housing estates of Rayners Lane was Alexandra Avenue, and with it came a spacious new shopping centre. A view from around 1938.

The Grosvenor Cinema, Rayners Lane, c.1937. The entertainment needs of the new suburb were well catered for at the Grosvenor Cinema, an art-deco masterpiece designed by F.E. Bromige, which opened in October 1936. In addition to films, there were live variety shows and there was a tea room. The cinema was at various times known as The Odeon, The Gaumont and latterly, The Ace. With its incredible "elephant's trunk" motif, it is a listed building, and in a new role as a night club, its original name, The Grosvenor, has been restored. (Tony Moss Collection)

Six

Roxeth and South Harrow

Roxeth Corner from Northolt Road, c.1908. This was the old village centre of Roxeth at the foot of Roxeth Hill, see page 41. Two of the village pubs can be seen here; the gabled Half Moon on the corner of Middle Road which has changed little externally in nearly 90 years. On the right, The Timber Carriage dispensed Clutterbuck's Fine Ales, and was rebuilt in the 1930s. The row of shops, including a branch of W.H. Cullen, were built in the front gardens of older cottages. All were rebuilt in the 1960s. The greenery on the left fronted the farmlands of The Grange.

Northolt Road looking towards Roxeth Corner, c.1904. These old shops and cottages disappeared in the early 1960s, as modern flats were constructed along Northolt Road. Alma Road, seen on the right, no longer exists. The new pavement on the left, was in front of Roxeth Parish Hall, site of the high rise Templar House.

Northolt Road looking towards Roxeth Corner, c.1912. So extensive have been the alterations to this road from the 1960s, that almost everything shown here has gone including, on the left, The Three Horseshoes pub, first licensed in 1730.

Northolt Road opposite the gas works, c.1907. Blocks of flats replaced these old terraces in the early 1960s.

Redevelopment of Northolt Road proceeding apace in September 1961, as new council flats rise behind half demolished terraces.

Northolt Road from South Harrow station, c.1912. The shops on the right have so far survived the rebuilding of Northolt Road, but all else has gone including the gas works, centre of picture. A new Waitrose superstore is being built there.

Northolt Road, by Sherwood Road, 1961. This grim landscape was soon to disappear but the huge gas holder, built in 1931, was to linger on until demolition in 1987, when few mourned its passing.

The extension of the District Railway line from Ealing Common to South Harrow opened on 28 June 1903, and offered a fast electric railway service through to Westminster and the City. A further extension to Uxbridge opened on 1 March 1910. In those early days, off peak traffic was sparse, and a single car service would be sufficient. This was a "B" class unit at Sudbury Town Station, c.1911.

Old South Harrow Station was in South Hill Avenue, and photographed in 1932 after the District service had been transferred to Piccadilly Line operation. The new station, with its Northolt Road entrance opened on 5 July 1935, but the old building survives today at the end of the up platform. (London Transport Museum)

An "S.T." type General bus in South Hill Avenue, c.1932. This was a terminus of local route 114a. On the left, at the corner of Northolt Road, was one of the sales offices for the vast Nash housing estate at Rayners Lane (freehold houses from £595). Note the billboard, very evocative of the early thirties. The Constellation pub was later built there.

Miles of open countryside were made easily accessible for Londoners following the opening of the new electric railway and, encouraged by attractive posters like this, a trip to rural Middlesex made an enjoyable day out. A "Cheap Sunday Return" cost 10d. (about 4p) from Piccadilly Circus to South Harrow.

Assembling for Tea at the Paddocks, Roxeth.

A day in the countryside was enhanced by a visit to one of the local pleasure resorts, the most popular of which was A. B. Champniss's Paddocks Sports Ground, the former Grove Dairy Farm in Northolt Road, Roxeth. Paddocks was a childrens favourite with fairground attractions and a miniature steam railway in its 30 acres. Here we see children assembling for tea at the huge canteen that could accommodate 2000 people. (A. & M. Back Collection)

Rambling in the Paddock Grounds. Roxeth.

Some of Harrow's bright young things strolling in the grounds of Paddocks, c.1912. Almost everyone wore a hat in those days. In the background, a range of swing boats and a small roundabout can be seen. The Paddocks grounds were incorporated into Alexandra Park in the 1930s, and a long row of shops was built along the Northolt Road frontage. It all looked much more fun in the Paddocks era!

Parkfield Road, c.1908. The arrival of the new District Railway at South Harrow gave impetus to housing developments near the station. This was the newly built Parkfield Road from Northolt Road showing vacant sites awaiting the new shopping parades.

Building a haystack at Parker's Farm, Roxeth, c.1912. Rural scenes like this could be seen at Roxeth well into the century. Stroud Gate was built on these old farmlands.

Northolt Road, c.1930. By the 1920s, rural Roxeth was rapidly changing into suburban South Harrow, with a large shopping centre to serve the new communities.

Northolt Road from South Harrow Station, c.1930. Another view of the South Harrow shopping centre in its early days, with sunblinds protecting the window displays.

South Vale, Sudbury Hill, c.1912. A pleasant by-way off Greenford Road leading to the Mount Park Estate and South Harrow. This is one of Harrow's most desirable residential areas, but according to the message on this postcard, it was not always so ... "The roads are laid out, but the plots don't sell".

Sudbury Hill Station

Sudbury Hill District Railway Station, was a corrugated iron structure in a muddy lane when photographed, c.1908. A fine new station designed by Charles Holden was built in 1932, when the service was transferred to Piccadilly Line operation.

G.C.R. South Harrow Station.

The Great Central Railway Station, Sudbury Hill, opened in 1906 and was also named "South Harrow", in spite of being some three quarters of a mile from the District Line's "South Harrow" Station. Two stations with the same name in different parts of the area obviously led to much confusion, which lasted until 19 July 1926, when the name was changed to Sudbury Hill. This photograph was taken c.1912 and shows South Vale on the right, and a sign pointing to the District Line station at Sudbury Hill, see page 171.

South Harrow (Sudbury Hill) Station, c.1908. A view from the bridge over Greenford Road, with the fields leading towards Mount Park Estate on the right.

Greenford Road from South Vale, c.1912. Many of these houses still stand, but the road is wider now to accommodate the relentless through traffic.

Greenford Road, c.1911. A delightful scene that has changed out of all recognition, the tree shaded lane having given way to a raging main road, with 1930s shops and a service road on the left, and the houses of Gainsborough Gardens to the right.

Seven
Around the Borough

The wide variety of railway links to central London ensured the popularity of Harrow as a residential area. This was another of them, the Watford Extension of the Baker Street and Waterloo Railway (Bakerloo Line), seen here c.1925 with one of the tube trains running through as yet undeveloped countryside between Kenton and Wealdstone. There were stations at Harrow & Wealdstone, Headstone Lane, and Hatch End.

With Best Wishes · 1908 ·

Kenton — Harrow —

R. Bros. B 42.

Kenton, to the east of Harrow, was an isolated hamlet surrounded by miles of farmland when this photograph was taken in 1908.

The Rest Hotel, Kenton Road, c.1908. With its picturesque tea gardens, the Rest was popular with cyclists and ramblers attracted by the unspoilt countryside. It was known as The Kenton Hotel in the 1920s, and was rebuilt in 1933. It is now familiar as The Travellers Rest, a prominent feature of Kenton's shopping centre, which grew up around it.

Headstone Manor, c.1912. This modest frontage conceals an ancient timber framed Manor House that dates in part from 1345, when it was owned by the Archbishops of Canterbury. Headstone is reputed to be even older than this and Archbishop Becket is said to have stayed there in 1170. Ownership passed to King Henry VIII in 1545. Headstone was a working farm through the centuries, and is now owned by the London Borough of Harrow. A programme of restoration is under way at this venerable building.

Headstone Manor and the Tithe Barn, c.1930. The barn dates from the sixteenth century, and has been restored to create a lively and interesting local museum.

The Moat, Headstone Manor, showing the two sixteenth-century barns in what was then a working farm.

Headstone Recreation Ground, Harrow

146269

Headstone Manor Recreation Ground, c.1935. The extensive farmlands of Headstone Manor became a public park in 1932.

The Dominion Cinema, Station Road, c.1937. By the middle of the 1930s, there were few undeveloped sites along Station Road between Harrow and Wealdstone. One of the last of them was Greenhill Farm, which eventually gave its site for the "wildly futuristic" Dominion Cinema, designed by F.E. Bromige. Later, when art-deco architecture such as this became unfashionable, this remarkable exterior was covered in blue metal cladding, and it stands in this state today. In 1995, the cinema was renamed The Safari, and it now specialises in Asian films. (Tony Moss Collection)

Wealdstone

The New Board School

I got time, Social's etc are very slow here this year plays at Watford are all right our treat push last Saturday with kind regards to all I remain yours F. G.

The Wrench Series No.

Bridge School, Wealdstone, photographed when new in 1902. The adjoining streets were named after famous poets which earned the locality the nickname "Poets Corner". These streets, together with the school, were replaced in 1970 with Harrow's new Civic Centre.

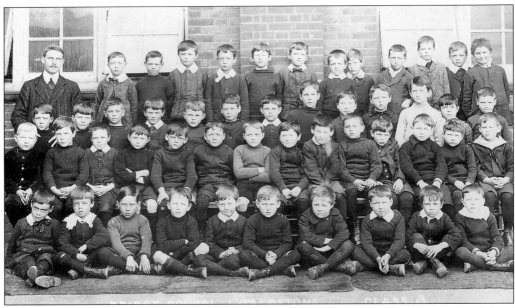

A class group at Bridge School, c.1907. This postcard was one produced by that most prolific of photographers, F.C. Hebblewhite of 136 High Street, Wealdstone. The legacy of Hebblewhite's work gives us an unrivalled picture of Edwardian Wealdstone, and his photography at local events was always on sale in postcard form the next day.

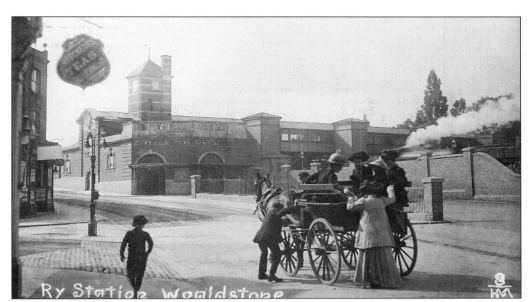

"Off for the day", c.1912. Willing hands help this lady climb aboard the horse-brake parked opposite the newly rebuilt Harrow & Wealdstone LNWR Station. Masons Avenue is on the left.

Harrow & Wealdstone Station, c.1912, as rebuilt with its clock tower seen on the left. The railway arrived here as early as 1837, the station was then merely called "Harrow" until it acquired its present name in 1897. The name "Station Road" refers to this station and not the later one at Greenhill (Harrow-on-the-Hill).

The Harrow & Wealdstone Rail Disaster, 8 October 1952. Harrow become the focus of world news on this tragic autumn morning as a local Tring to Euston train at platform 4 was struck from behind by the Perth to London Express travelling at 55 mph. By sheer misfortune, a Euston to Liverpool Express was approaching at 60 mph on an adjacent line as the wreckage spilled into its track causing a second major collision. All three trains were completely wrecked with a pile of smashed carriages 30 ft high. The shock of this massive impact stopped the station clock high in its tower at 8.19 am. 122 people died in the disaster. (Hulton Deutsch Collection)

Under the watchful eye of the shop manager, a pack of W. H. Smith & Sons paper boys, complete with company caps, prepare for their deliveries from the Wealdstone shop at Station Buildings, c.1908.

Wealdstone's shops at the corner of High Street and Masons Avenue, c.1912, showing the well stocked premises of T. Brainsby (grocer), J. Gilham (baker & confectioner), and G.C. Hill (tobacconist & hairdresser).

Wealdstone High Street, by Canning Road, c.1912. Always a lively shopping area, this view shows Smith's hardware stores crammed with goods of all kinds. Adjacent are the familiar chain stores of Home & Colonial and W.H. Cullen. Wenham's (newsagents) displays an advertisement for a vanished newspaper, the Wealdstone Observer.

A smart turnout of staff in aprons and waistcoats at W.H. Cullen's shop, Wealdstone, c.1908.

The start of Middlesex Athletic Club's seven-and-three-quarter miles walking race from the club's Masons Avenue headquarters, 16 March 1912. Members of North London Harriers, Ashcombe A.C. and Queens Park Harriers also competed in the race which was won by world record holder H.V. Ross of Middlesex A.C.

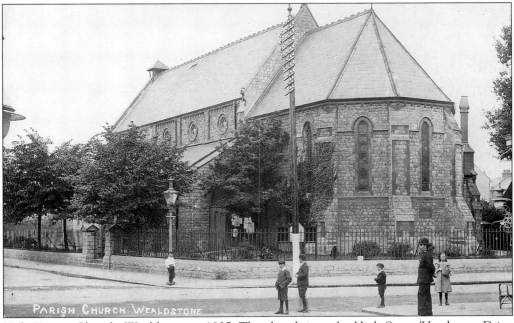

Holy Trinity Church, Wealdstone, c.1905. The church is at the High Street/Headstone Drive corner, and was consecrated in June 1881.

The Case is Altered, High Street, Wealdstone, c.1907. This old pub was soon to be overshadowed by a new neighbour, the Magistrates Court, built in 1908 on the site of cottages to the left of this picture. The pub itself was eventually rebuilt, but the large forecourt was retained, and still exists.

The Case is Altered with the Magistrates Court, c.1910. This is now Wealdstone Police Station. The scale of Wealdstone's newer buildings when compared with the older ones is well caught here.

The Parisian Bioscope, c.1909. With an exotic name not matched by its architecture, Wealdstone's cinema stood at the Graham Road/High Street corner. Note the outside pay box. The message on this card was written in April 1910 ... "This is our Hall, how do you like it?"

By 1911, the Bioscope had acquired domes, columns, an intricate frieze, and a new name, The Wealdstone Cinema.

The Bright Lights of Wealdstone, 1911 style. The Wealdstone Cinema ablaze with electric light, was a dramatic sight in the dimly gas-lit High Street. A film of the Coronation procession of King George V and Queen Mary was showing when this photograph was taken.

Wealdstone celebrated the Coronation on 22 June 1911 with much enthusiasm. There were decorated streets, a fancy dress parade, and a children's service at the local school. This was the "Coronation Villa", erected in the recreation ground and ceremonially burnt down after dark to the accompaniment of a firework display.

The Children's Coronation Service Rehearsal, High Street schools, 21 June 1911. This was the day before the Coronation, and 2000 children (apparently) gathered in the school playground for a final rehearsal of their singing.

Coronation Day, with the children's service going well. The children have been joined by a brass band and a good selection of onlookers, including a fireman on horse back. The school, at the corner of Grant Road, dates from 1883, and is currently the site of Wealdstone Branch Library.

H.M. Stationery Office, Headstone Drive, c.1930, a fine building once occupied by David Allan's, the printers. Harrow Crown Court is here now. To the left can be seen the chimneys of the Kodak factories, the largest industrial plant in the borough. Kodak established these works in 1891, and has expanded to occupy 55 acres with a workforce of around 5000.

Three men and dog preside over a far more modest business, the Wealdstone Paper Co., Byron Road Works, c.1907. There were no paper banks in those days!

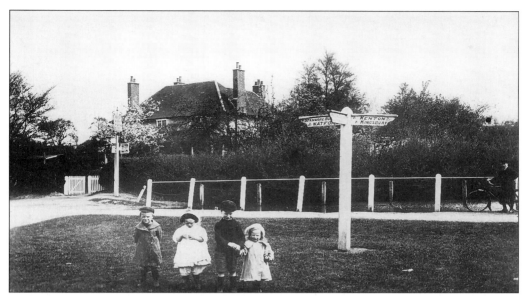

The Duck in the Pond, Kenton Lane, c.1909. There is now a busy crossroads here, and although the pub is still thriving, the pond with its ducks has long gone.

Kenton Lane, c.1918. This is now a busy main road linking Kenton with Harrow Weald and Belmont.

The sight of the Seven Balls pub, Kenton Lane would have been very welcome to the drivers of these "B" type buses on route 58 after the long dusty haul from Charing Cross via Edgware Road and Stanmore, c.1912. These buses were operated by London General Omnibus Co., forerunner of London Transport.

The first motor buses in the Harrow area were those operated from July 1906 by London & North Western Railway on their route from Watford Station to Harrow & Wealdstone Station. This Milnes-Daimler bus was photographed c.1907. Few buses carried route numbers in those early days.

BROCKHURST CORNER   HARROW WEALD.

Brockhurst Corner, Harrow Weald, 1914. A Daimler motor bus owned by Metropolitan Electric Tramways is seen working the short-lived route 173, Watford to South Harrow Station. Following the outbreak of was in 1914, many of these double deckers were sent to France and Belgium and used as troop carriers in the battlefields.

HARROW WEALD

High Road, Harrow Weald, c.1913, showing P.J. Walk's Refreshment Rooms, W.F. Smith (butcher), and Wilcox & Sons (fruiterers).

Harrow-on-the-Hill, c.1890.

Acknowledgements

For their kindness in allowing me to use photographs from their collections in this book, I gratefully acknowledge the help given by Margaret and Arthur Back, Tony Moss, London Transport Museum, and Hulton Deutsch Collection. Special thanks are also due to transport historian David Brewster, and to Lens of Sutton.